MICHIGAN TRAVEL GUIDE 2023

Zelia Turnock

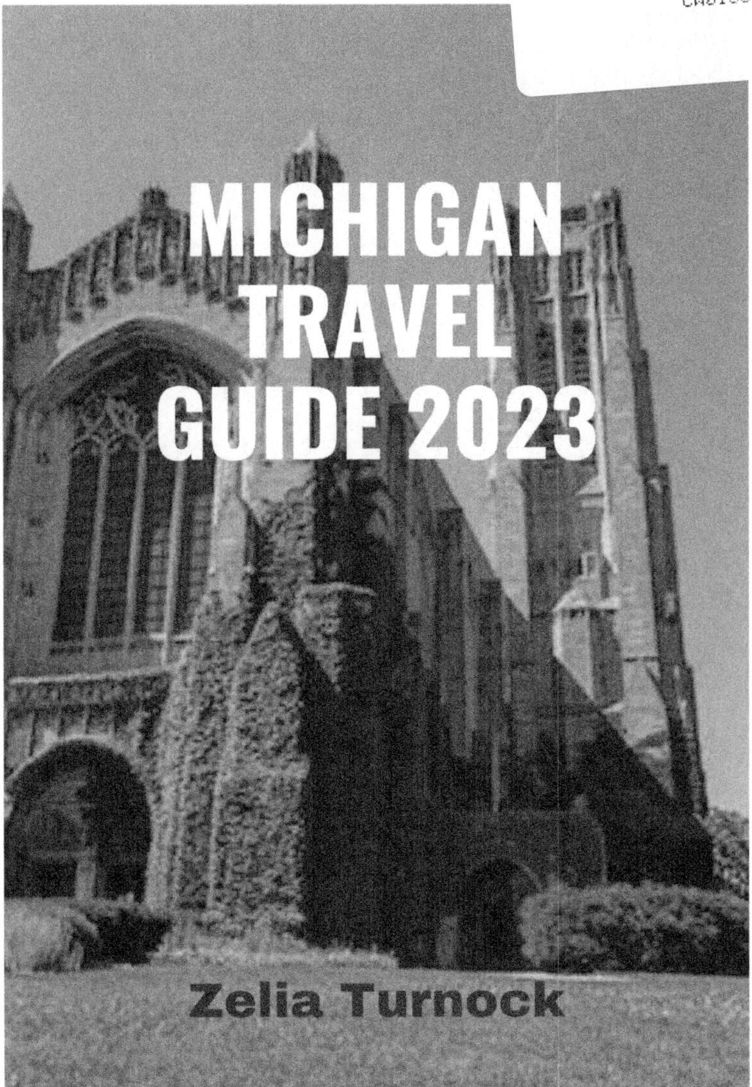

MICHIGAN TRAVEL GUIDE 2023:

Exploring Michigan's Charm From City Lights to Lakeshore Delights

By

Zelia Turnock

TABLE OF CONTENTS

Introduction

Thank you for purchasing this book. Michigan is a wonderful place to visit! We are delighted to have you along for this captivating journey through the Great Lakes State's wonders. Whether you're an enthusiastic globe-trotter, an inquisitive traveler, or essentially looking for a brilliant departure, this book is your key to opening the fortunes of Michigan.

Prepare to be engulfed by stunning landscapes, bustling metropolises, and charming small towns that will win your heart. From the sandy shores of the Incomparable Lakes to the glorious wild of the Upper Promontory, Michigan's magnificence exceeds all rational limitations.

You will discover delightful anecdotes, insider advice, and hidden gems that will make your travel experience truly unforgettable as you flip through these pages. Enjoy delectable regional cuisine, take in the rich history and culture that make Michigan a one-of-a-kind destination, and be inspired by the warm hospitality of the locals.

This helpful guide is here to make your trip enjoyable and hassle-free, whether you're planning a weekend getaway, a trip with the family, or a solo adventure. Thus, gather your sacks, hold nothing back from new encounters, and let the "Michigan Travel Guide" be your handy dandy buddy on this amazing endeavor.

Prepared to leave on a remarkable odyssey? We should start our experience together and gain experiences that will endure forever. Michigan's captivating world is waiting for you!

My First Visitation to Michigan

My First Visitation to Michigan During my enriching six months in Michigan, I embarked on a once-in-a-lifetime adventure that will never be forgotten and will forever remain in my heart. I was captivated by the breathtaking landscapes, warm hospitality, and plethora of experiences waiting to be discovered from the moment I arrived in the Great Lakes State.

My process started in the dynamic city of Detroit, where I drenched myself in the city's rich history and social legacy. I investigated the Detroit Establishment of Expressions, wondered about the shocking engineering of the Watchman Building, and appreciated the luscious kinds of the city's assorted culinary scene. The Motown Exhibition hall was a specific feature, taking me back in time through the deep rhythms that characterized a period.

I moved north to the Upper Peninsula's serene beauty as I continued my exploration. I was awestruck by the picture-perfect shores of Lake Superior and the majestic Pictured Rocks National Lakeshore. Climbing through lavish timberlands and seeing the great cascades, I felt really associated with nature in its most perfect structure.

Another treasure I enjoyed seeing was Mackinac Island. Missing vehicles, the island's pony drawn carriages and bikes offered a nostalgic appeal as I investigated the noteworthy Stronghold Mackinac and enjoyed the island's renowned fudge.

I was greeted with the friendliness and warmth of Michiganders throughout my stay. Local people were consistently prepared to share their number one spots, suggest the best diners, and give bits of knowledge into the state's rich social legacy. The modest communities I experienced en route, similar to Holland and Cross City, felt like a usual hangout spot with their inviting climate.

I ended up captivated by the occasional marvels Michigan brought to the table. When I went to the apple orchards and cider mills in the fall, the landscape changed into a kaleidoscope of colors, which made my visit truly magical. The colder time of year brought snow-loaded scenes and the chance to encounter exciting outside exercises like skiing and snowboarding.

I witnessed nature's revival as spring blossomed, with the state's botanical gardens bursting with vibrant blooms. Furthermore, when summer showed up, the sandy sea shores of Lake Michigan called, offering an ideal reprieve from the warm days.

All through my excursion, the "Michigan Travel Guide" ended up being an important friend, giving smart tips, unlikely treasures, and viable counsel that advanced my encounters.

I learned the value of exploration, connection, and embracing the beauty of the world around us during my six-month stay in Michigan, which was a transformative adventure. I leave with valued recollections, new kinships, and a profound appreciation for the miracles that Michigan brings to the table. Michigan, thank you for an unforgettable journey until we meet again.

Brief History of Michigan

Native American civilizations, European exploration, territorial disputes, and the rise of industrialization are all woven into

Michigan's fascinating history. We should dig into the long and nitty gritty excursion that molded the Incomparable Lakes State.

Native Americans who live there:
Well before European pilgrims showed up, Michigan's territories were possessed by different Local American clans. The northern regions were dominated by Algonquian-speaking peoples like the Anishinaabe (Ojibwe), Odawa, and Potawatomi, while the southern regions were populated by the Wyandot (Huron) and Miami. Fishing, hunting, and farming were the main means by which these indigenous peoples made a living, and their rich cultures were a big part of Michigan's early history.

Exploration and Settlement in Europe:
The appearance of European pilgrims denoted another part of Michigan's set of experiences. In 1610, French voyager

Étienne Brûlé became perhaps the earliest European to arrive at the area, trailed by Samuel de Champlain and other French brokers. The French made a case for the locale and laid out four general stores, fashioning coalitions with Local American clans to extend their impact.

In 1668, Father Jacques Marquette and Louis Jolliet investigated and planned the district, opening up new open doors for exchange and settlement. Their campaigns prepared for French preachers and fur brokers to lay out posts along the shores of the Incomparable Lakes.

English Control and American Transformation:
The English dealt with Michigan in the wake of overcoming the French in the Seven Years' Conflict (1756-1763). Following the American Unrest, the district turned into a piece of the recently free US through the Settlement of Paris in 1783. But Britain kept

control of important forts in the territory, like Fort Detroit.

Michigan as a Region:
With Detroit as its capital, the Michigan Territory was officially established in 1805. The domain experienced huge development during this period, with a deluge of pioneers pulled in by the ripe land and plentiful normal assets.

War of 1812:
Michigan was a significant battleground for the United States and Great Britain during the War of 1812. Post Detroit was given up to the English in 1812 yet was subsequently recovered by American powers in 1813. The contention further cemented American command over the locale.

Statehood and the Toledo War:
Michigan's excursion to statehood was not without challenges. In 1835, a limited debate known as the "Toledo War" emitted

between Michigan and the territory of Ohio over the city of Toledo and the Toledo Strip. When Congress gave Michigan statehood in 1837, it gave up its claims to the Toledo Strip to end the conflict. On January 26, 1837, Michigan turned into the 26th state in the Association.

Industrialization and Development:
The lumber industry, mining, and manufacturing all contributed to Michigan's rapid industrialization during the nineteenth century. The revelation of copper in the Upper Promontory and iron metal in the Marquette and Menominee areas energized financial development, drawing in floods of outsiders looking for thriving.

The car business likewise assumed a critical part in molding Michigan's character. The introduction of the assembly line by Henry Ford at the beginning of the 20th century revolutionized manufacturing and made automobiles more affordable and accessible.

Detroit, known as the "Engine City," turned into the focal point of the auto business, drawing in specialists from the nation over.

Social and Political Change:
Michigan was at the forefront of social and political change throughout the 20th century. The work development picked up speed, and laborers battled for better working circumstances and fair wages. Rosa Parks and other prominent figures contributed to the fight for racial equality during the civil rights movement, which was marked by both significant difficulties and progress.

Present-day Michigan:
Today, Michigan remains a different and dynamic state, known for its regular excellence, modern legacy, and social commitments. The Great Lakes are still an essential resource that supports businesses, tourism, and leisure activities. The state stays a center point for auto producing, and

its colleges and research foundations add to headways in different fields.

Michigan's set of experiences is a demonstration of the strength and versatility of its kin, from the native clans who previously possessed the land to the pioneers and foreigners who molded its turn of events. The tradition of Michigan's past keeps on affecting its present and promises an astonishing future for a long time into the future.

The people of Michigan and its cultural landmarks

The people of Michigan, often referred to as "Michiganders" or "Michiganians," are known for their warm hospitality, resilience, and diverse cultural heritage. With a population representing a wide array of ethnic backgrounds, Michigan is a melting pot of traditions and customs that contribute to its vibrant and inclusive society.

Ethnic Diversity:
Michigan's population is ethnically diverse, with a rich tapestry of cultural backgrounds. The state has a significant population of European descent, including individuals with Polish, German, Irish, Italian, and Dutch heritage. Detroit, in particular, has historically been home to a large African American community, contributing significantly to the city's cultural fabric.

Michigan's Native American heritage remains an essential part of its identity, with several federally recognized tribes calling the state home. The Ojibwe (Anishinaabe), Odawa, and Potawatomi have a deep-rooted presence in the northern regions, while the Saginaw Chippewa and the Grand Traverse Band of Ottawa and Chippewa Indians reside in the Lower Peninsula.

Immigrant Communities:

Throughout Michigan's history, waves of immigrants have settled in the state, enriching its cultural landscape. The early 20th century saw an influx of immigrants from Eastern Europe, including Poland, Ukraine, and Russia, adding to the diversity of the state's population.

The Arab American community also plays a prominent role in Michigan's cultural fabric, with a significant population of Lebanese, Yemeni, and Iraqi descent. Dearborn, a suburb of Detroit, is known for having one of the largest Arab American populations in the United States.

Cultural Landmarks:

Michigan boasts a plethora of cultural landmarks that showcase its diverse heritage and history. Detroit, as the state's largest city, is home to numerous iconic sites, including the Detroit Institute of Arts, renowned for its extensive collection of artwork, including pieces by Vincent van Gogh and Diego Rivera.

The Motown Museum, located in Detroit, pays tribute to the legendary Motown record label, which played a pivotal role in shaping American popular music. Visitors can explore the recording studio where artists like Stevie Wonder, Diana Ross, and The Jackson 5 recorded some of their biggest hits.

Mackinac Island, a unique cultural landmark, preserves its Victorian charm, prohibiting the use of motor vehicles and allowing visitors to step back in time. The island's Grand Hotel, a historic icon, offers a glimpse into the past with its architecture and grandeur.

The Henry Ford Museum and Greenfield Village in Dearborn provide an immersive experience in American history and innovation, showcasing artifacts and exhibits related to the country's industrial and technological progress.

In addition to these landmarks, Michigan is home to several festivals and events that celebrate its diverse cultural heritage. The Tulip Time Festival in Holland, Michigan, honors the area's Dutch heritage with vibrant tulip displays, parades, and traditional Dutch dancing.

Festivals like the Ann Arbor Art Fair and the Detroit Jazz Festival draw crowds from around the country, celebrating art, music, and creative expression.

Sports and Recreation:
Sports also play a significant role in Michigan's culture, with passionate fan bases supporting professional sports teams like the Detroit Lions (NFL), Detroit Tigers (MLB), Detroit Pistons (NBA), and Detroit Red Wings (NHL).

Recreation is an integral part of life in Michigan, with the state offering diverse outdoor activities. The Great Lakes and numerous inland lakes provide opportunities for boating, fishing, and water sports, while the state's extensive park system allows for hiking, camping, and exploring the natural beauty.

In conclusion, the people of Michigan reflect the state's rich cultural diversity and welcoming spirit. Michigan's cultural landmarks celebrate its heritage and history, while its vibrant communities continue to shape the state's identity through its traditions, arts, and celebrations. From the bustling city life of Detroit to the serene beauty of its natural landscapes, Michigan's people and their cultural landmarks make the state a unique and captivating destination.

Best time to Visit Michigan

Michigan's magnificence and attractions are assorted over time, offering remarkable encounters in each season. The best opportunity to visit Michigan generally relies upon individual inclinations, wanted exercises, and the sort of involvement one looks for. Let's take a look at each season to help you plan your trip:

1.   March through May:
In Michigan, spring brings a flurry of color and new life. As the snow dissolves, the scenes wake up with blossoming blossoms and growing trees. The weather can be unpredictable, with temperatures ranging from cold to pleasant. Spring is a brilliant time for open-air exercises like climbing in the many state parks, visiting greenhouses,

and investigating the blooming cherry plantations in Cross City.

2.	Summer (June to August):
Summer is without a doubt the pinnacle traveler season in Michigan. The weather conditions are warm, and the state's streams become a jungle gym for beachgoers and water devotees. The Incomparable Lakes and inland lakes offer sufficient chances for swimming, sailing, kayaking, and fishing. Summer is an exciting time to experience Michigan's cultural vibrancy thanks to festivals and events like the National Cherry Festival in Traverse City and the Tulip Time Festival in Holland.

3.	Fall (September to November):
The breathtaking beauty of Michigan's fall foliage has earned it a reputation. As the temperatures cool, the woods change into a kaleidoscope of dynamic tones. Fall is an ideal time for grand drives along tree-lined streets, climbing in the Upper Landmass to

observe the fall tones, and investigating apple plantations and pumpkin patches. During this time of year, a popular event is the Mackinac Bridge Walk on Labor Day, where pedestrians can cross the famous bridge.

4.   Winter: November through February
Michigan's winter season is a magical land of snow-covered landscapes and outdoor activities. With skiing, snowboarding, snowshoeing, and ice fishing opportunities, the state is a haven for fans of winter sports. Ice sculptures and winter festivals transform northern Michigan, including the cities of Charlevoix and Petoskey, into a winter wonderland. The snowmobiling trails in the Upper Peninsula are well-known, and visitors can take in the breathtaking frozen beauty of the Pictured Rocks National Lakeshore.

5.   Shoulder Seasons (Spring and Fall):

The shoulder times of spring and fall offer the upside of fewer groups and more reasonable facilities contrasted with the pinnacle mid-year months. The weather is generally pleasant during these times, making it ideal for outdoor activities without the heat of the summer or the cold of the winter.

The best time to visit Michigan ultimately depends on your preferences and interests. Summer is the obvious season for water sports enthusiasts and beachgoers. Make your trip in the fall if you want to see the stunning fall foliage. For people who appreciate winter sports and blanketed scenes, a colder time of year visit is great. On the other hand, if you like milder temperatures and fewer people, you might want to go during the shoulder seasons in the spring or fall.

Regardless of the time, Michigan's exceptional attractions and warm neighborliness guarantee a significant and enhancing experience for each explorer.

Michigan's climate conditions

Michigan's location in the Great Lakes creates a distinctive and varied weather pattern, which influences the state's climate. The state experiences all four seasons, each with its own charm and outdoor activities opportunities.

1. March through May:

Spring in Michigan is a time of change, set apart by softening snow and climbing temperatures. The weather conditions can be eccentric, with fluctuating temperatures and infrequent downpour showers. Rivers and streams expand as the snow melts, and the landscapes come to life with blossoming plants and trees. Normal temperatures range from 40°F (4°C) to 60°F (15°C) in Spring and move to 50°F (10°C) to 70°F (21°C) in May. Spring is an incredible time for climbing, birdwatching, and visiting professional flowerbeds.

2. Summer (June to August):

Michigan shines during the summer, which is its busiest tourist season. With average temperatures ranging from 70°F (21°C) to 80°F (27°C), the weather is pleasant and warm. However, in July and August, temperatures occasionally reach 90°F (30°C). The Incomparable Lakes and inland lakes offer reviving swimming open doors, and the sandy seashores entice guests to unwind and loll in the sun. Summer is ideal for boating, kayaking, and other watersports. Celebrations, open-air shows, and occasions make Michigan an astonishing and dynamic objective during this season.

3.   September through November:

Fall in Michigan is renowned for its fabulous foliage as the leaves change tones. In September, average temperatures range from 50°F (10°C) to 70°F (21°C), and in November, they range from 30°F (-1°C) to 50°F (10°C). This is followed by a gradual cooling of the weather. The state changes into a kaleidoscope of lively tints, making it an ideal time for grand drives, climbing, and photography. In addition, you can go to apple orchards, pumpkin patches, and harvest festivals and events in the fall.

4.   Winter (December to February):

Winter in Michigan is frigid, particularly in the northern locales and the Upper Landmass. In January, the average temperature ranges from 20°F (-7°C) to 30°F (-1°C). The state receives a lot of snow, making it ideal for winter sports like ice fishing, snowmobiling, skiing, and snowboarding. The Incomparable Lakes assume a huge part in impacting Michigan's colder time of year environment, as they can produce lake-impact snow, prompting restricted weighty snowfall in specific regions.

5. Seasons of transition (Spring and Fall):
Temperature swings are common during the spring and fall transitional seasons. As Michigan sits between the directing impact of the Incomparable Lakes and mainland air masses, temperature varieties can be very sensational during these seasons. It's prudent to dress in layers to oblige changing weather patterns.

While Michigan's environment shifts consistently, its unmistakable four seasons give a different scope of encounters for inhabitants and guests the same. Whether you're investigating the bright fall foliage, partaking in the warm mid-year days on the oceanfront, embracing the colder time of year wonderland, or seeing the enlivening of nature in spring, Michigan's environment conditions guarantee a vital and consistently evolving experience.

The Geography of Michigan

The Great Lakes, rivers, forests, dunes, and rolling hills are just some of the natural landscapes that make up Michigan's remarkably diverse geography. The state is divided into two distinct peninsulas and is situated in the United States Great Lakes region: the Lower Promontory and the

Upper Landmass. How about we investigate the geology of Michigan exhaustively:

1.   Incredible Lakes:
Michigan is frequently alluded to as the "Incomparable Lakes State" because its remarkable geology is overwhelmed by four of the five Extraordinary Lakes: Lake Predominant, Lake Michigan, Lake Huron, and Lake Erie. These huge freshwater lakes give various open doors to amusement, transportation, and the travel industry. Lake Michigan, situated toward the west of the Lower Landmass, flaunts sandy sea shores, beachfront hills, and clear waters, drawing in beachgoers and water lovers. The Waterways of Mackinac interface Lake Michigan and Lake Huron and are crossed by the notable Mackinac Scaffold, connecting the two landmasses.

2.   Lower Landmass:
There are vast tracts of farmland, rolling hills, and dense forests in the fertile Lower

Peninsula of Michigan. The Lower Peninsula's northern regions experience cooler temperatures due to their proximity to the Great Lakes, whereas the southern portion has a more temperate climate. The Lower Peninsula is home to important cities like Detroit, Lansing, Grand Rapids, and Ann Arbor. The state's capital, Lansing, sits in the southern piece of the Lower Landmass and is home to the Michigan State Legislative Hall and a few colleges.

3.   Upper Landmass:
Isolated from the Lower Landmass by the Waterways of Mackinac, the Upper Promontory (UP) of Michigan is less populated and known for its rough and wild territory. It is lined by Lake Better to the north, Lake Michigan toward the south, and Lake Huron toward the east. The UP is a heaven for nature darlings, with huge woods, pleasant cascades, and flawless lakes. The Porcupine Mountains in the western piece of the UP offer amazing vistas

and testing climbing trails. In the past, the region was home to significant mining operations for iron ore and copper.

4. Forests:

The vast forests that cover Michigan cover nearly half of the state's land area. The Lower Landmass is essentially made out of hardwood woodlands, including species like oak, maple, beech, and cherry. Coniferous forests with pine, spruce, and fir trees dominate the northern parts of the Lower Peninsula and Upper Peninsula.

5. Sand Rises:

The western shore of Michigan's Lower Landmass is renowned for its staggering sand rises. The Resting Bear Hills Public Lakeshore along Lake Michigan is perhaps the most notorious and pleasant area in the state. These wind- and water-shaped dunes offer unique landscapes for hiking, dune climbing, and taking in the lake from above.

6.   Inland Lakes and Waterways:
Michigan's abundance of inland lakes and rivers makes it particularly appealing to outdoor enthusiasts. The state flaunts more than 11,000 inland lakes, making it a famous destination for fishing, drifting, and water sports. The scenic beauty of the Au Sable, Manistee, and Muskegon rivers, in addition to their excellent fishing opportunities, have earned them widespread recognition.

7.   Islands:
Michigan has numerous islands in the Great Lakes in addition to its mainland. Mackinac Island, situated in the Waterways of Mackinac, is a famous vacation location known for its notable engineering, horse-drawn carriages, and the renowned Stupendous Lodging. Isle Royale, arranged in Lake Prevalent, is an assigned public park and a shelter for explorers and wild fans.

In conclusion, Michigan's geography is a beautiful mix of lakes, forests, dunes, and beautiful landscapes that offer a wide range of cultural and recreational activities. Whether investigating the sandy shores of Lake Michigan, climbing through the unblemished wild of the Upper Promontory, or wondering about the glory of the Incomparable Lakes, Michigan's assorted topography guarantees there is something for each nature sweetheart and traveler.

CHAPTER 1

Planning Your Trip to Michigan

Michigan is a state in the Incomparable Lakes district of the upper Midwestern US. With its long history of transportation and assembling, Michigan is known as the "Car Capital of the World". Nonetheless, Michigan is likewise a condition of regular excellence, with its numerous lakes, timberlands, and rises.

Michigan has a lot to offer, including trips to Mackinac Island and the Sleeping Bear Dunes National Lakeshore for hiking. Here are some ways to design your outing to Michigan:

When to leave: The ideal time to visit Michigan depends on your interests because it has four distinct seasons. Summer is the most famous chance to visit, as the weather conditions are warm and radiant.

Notwithstanding, the fall foliage is additionally gorgeous in Michigan, and the cold weather months offer open doors for skiing and other winter sports.

Where to go: There are numerous extraordinary spots to visit in Michigan, yet the following are a couple of the most famous:

Mackinac Island: This vehicle-free island is a famous vacationer location, known for its notable Terrific Lodging and lovely view.

National Park Sleeping Bear Dunes: This park is home to the absolute most lovely rises in the US.

Envisioned Rocks Public Lakeshore: This park is known for its vivid sandstone precipices and dazzling perspectives on Lake Unrivaled.

Detroit: The state's biggest city, Detroit is home to the Henry Portage Gallery, the Motown Exhibition Hall, and other social attractions.

Michigan City: This city is situated in the core of Michigan's wine country, and is an extraordinary spot to visit for outside exercises, like climbing, trekking, and drifting.

In Ann Arbor: This school town is home to the College of Michigan and is an incredible spot to visit for its dynamic expressions scene and various cafés.

Step-by-step instructions to get around: Michigan has a decent arrangement of thruways and highways, so it is not difficult to get around via vehicle. Notwithstanding, there are likewise numerous public transportation choices accessible, like transport, trains, and ships.

Stay where: Michigan has numerous excellent lodging options, including bed and breakfasts, cabins, and hotels. There are also a lot of cheap campgrounds to choose from.

What to pack: The time of year you visit Michigan will determine the kind of clothing you need to bring. Notwithstanding, a few basics incorporate agreeable shoes, sunscreen, shades, a cap, and a waterproof shell.

Arranging your agenda: You can begin planning your itinerary once you have decided where you want to go. You can customize your trip to Michigan by exploring it in a variety of ways. For instance, if you are keen on history, you could visit the Henry Portage Gallery and Greenfield Town. You could hike in the Sleeping Bear Dunes National Lakeshore or go to Pictured Rocks National Lakeshore if you like nature.

Budgeting: Michigan is an inexpensive state to visit. Be that as it may, the expense of your outing will rely upon the exercises you decide to do and the spots you stay. Camping, making your meals, and going to free attractions are all great ways to cut costs if you're on a tight budget.

Getting to Michigan

The various ways to get to Michigan, along with some details about each, are as follows:

1.Via Plane

Michigan has three significant air terminals: Detroit Metro Air terminal (DTW), Lansing Capital Area Global Air terminal (LAN), and Diocesan Worldwide Air terminal (FNT). DTW is the biggest and most all-around associated air terminal in the state, and it is served by most significant carriers. Although LAN and FNT are smaller airports, they provide travelers from certain regions of the country with more convenient connections.

2. Via Train

Amtrak offers three train courses that serve Michigan: the Pere Marquette, the Blue Water, and the Wolverine is a rapid train that runs between Chicago and Pontiac, Michigan. The Blue Water line goes through Rock, Lansing, and Kalamazoo, and the Pere Marquette line stops in St Joseph, Holland, and Fabulous Rapids.

By Transport

Greyhound and Megabus offer transport administration to significant urban communities in Michigan. Greyhound is the more settled organization, while Megabus offers lower admissions.

3. Via Vehicle

Michigan is situated in the Midwest, and it is lined by four different states: Ohio, Illinois, Wisconsin, and Indiana I-94, I-75, I-69, and I-96 are the most important interstate highways that pass through Michigan.

Combination of Methods You can also travel to Michigan by combining different modes of transportation. For instance, you could fly into DTW and afterward lease a vehicle to head to your objective. Alternatively, you could take a bus to your final location after taking the train from Chicago to Detroit.

Cost Depending on how you get there, getting to Michigan will cost you differently. Flying is the most costly choice, while transport travel is the most reasonable. Vehicle rental is likewise a somewhat reasonable choice, particularly if you are going with a gathering.

Time

How much time it takes to get to Michigan will likewise fluctuate contingent upon the technique for transportation you pick. Flying is the quickest choice, while transport travel is the slowest. Vehicle travel is a decent split of the difference among speed and cost.

In general, traveling to Michigan is relatively simple. There are a few unique techniques for transportation accessible, and the expense of movement is sensible. You will be able to get to Michigan in a way that fits your needs and your budget, whether you drive, take the bus, take the train, or fly.

Here are a few extra ways to get to Michigan:

- Book your flights or train tickets ahead of time, particularly assuming you are going during the top season.

- If you want to explore Michigan at your own pace, think about renting a car.

- Take the train or bus if you're on a tight budget.

- Make certain to figure out the expense of stopping assuming you are heading to Michigan.

- Travel time should be plenty, especially if you're flying.

Michigan's Top Destinations

Michigan is a state with a ton to offer, from its dazzling Incredible Lakes coastline to its lavish woodlands and moving slopes. Here are a portion of the top objections in

Michigan that you won't have any desire to miss:

1. Mackinac Island is a vehicle-free island in the Waterways of Mackinac that is known for its noteworthy appeal, fudge shops, and delightful landscape. Guests can investigate the island by bicycle, by walking, or by horse-drawn carriage.

2. Resting Bear Ridges Public Lakeshore is a shocking stretch of shore in northwest Michigan that is home to transcending sand rises, flawless sea shores, and rich woods. In the park, visitors can camp, bike, swim, hike, and bike.

3. Envisioned Rocks Public Lakeshore is one more gorgeous stretch of shoreline in Michigan, this one situated in the eastern Upper Promontory. The recreation area is known for its bright sandstone bluffs, which ascend to 200 feet above Lake Prevalent. In the park, visitors can kayak, boat, and hike.

4. Henry Passage Gallery is a rambling historical center complex in Dearborn, Michigan, that is home to a tremendous assortment of curios and shows connected with American history, innovation, and culture. The Wright Brothers' first airplane, Rosa Parks' bus, and Thomas Edison's laboratory are all on display for visitors.

5. Isle Royale Public Park is a secluded island in Lake Better that is home to an assortment of untamed life, including moose, wolves, and bears. In the park, visitors can fish, camp, hike, and boat.

6. Cross City is a famous retreat town in northwest Michigan that is known for its wineries, seashores, and greens. Guests can likewise appreciate climbing, trekking, and kayaking nearby.

There are numerous art museums, breweries, and parks in Grand Rapids, a thriving city in western Michigan. In addition, the city offers nightlife, dining, and shopping to visitors.

Kitch-iti-kipi is a characteristic spring in the Upper Promontory that is known for its completely clear water and bright fish. Guests can take a boat visit through the spring or swim in the water.

These are only a couple of the numerous extraordinary objections in Michigan. Michigan is a state that has something for everyone thanks to its stunning scenery, extensive history, and vibrant culture.
Regardless of what you're searching for in a getaway, you're certain to track it down in Michigan. So begin arranging your outing today!

Clothing:

Since you'll probably be walking around and exploring, it's best to wear a mix of casual and comfortable clothing.

- Pack lightweight sweaters, shorts, and t-shirts for the summer.

- Layer up with a warm coat, scarf, gloves, and hat during the winter.

- If you're anticipating doing any outside exercises, pack suitable stuff, like climbing boots, swimwear, and a bathing suit.

Shoes:

Because you'll probably be walking around a lot, you'll need good walking shoes.

- Pack hiking boots with good traction in case you intend to hike.

- Pack sandals or water shoes if you plan to do any water sports.

Accessories:
Shades, sunscreen, and a cap are fundamental for safeguarding yourself from the sun.

- If you plan to spend a lot of time in the woods, insect repellent is also a good idea.

- If you are going on a trip during the rainy season, you should bring a poncho or rain jacket.

Toiletries:
- Pack your essential toiletries, including cleanser, conditioner, cleanser, toothpaste, and toothbrush.

- If you have any extraordinary necessities, like physician-endorsed meds, make certain to pack those too.

- Additionally, you may want to bring a first-aid kit in travel size.

Electronics:
- A cell phone is an unquestionable requirement for remaining associated and for taking pictures.

- A PC or tablet is likewise really smart on the off chance that you anticipate accomplishing any work or everyday life you're voyaging.

- If you're anticipating doing any outside exercises, you may likewise need to pack a camera, GPS, or other electronic gadgets.

This is only an essential pressing rundown, and you might have to change it relying upon your particular requirements and interests. Be that as it may, this ought to give you a decent beginning stage for arranging your excursion to Michigan.

Download a Michigan map for offline use

Downloading a Michigan map for disconnected use can be monstrously useful, particularly while you're heading out to regions with restricted or no web network. Whether you're arranging an excursion, investigating nature, or just exploring around the state, having a disconnected guide guarantees you will not get lost and can get to fundamental data in a hurry.

A Michigan map can be downloaded for offline use in several different ways:

1. **Google Guides:** Google Maps, the most widely used navigation app, provides an offline map feature. To download a Michigan map, open the Google Guides application on your gadget and quest for the ideal region in Michigan. When the region is apparent on your screen, type "Alright

guides" in the hunt bar and tap "Download" to save the guide for disconnected use. You can zoom in and out to choose the ideal inclusion region.

2.   Here WeGo: Here WeGo is yet another excellent offline map navigation app. You only need to go to the app store, download the Here WeGo app, search for Michigan, and pick the area you want to save. Then, at that point, tap the three dabs menu and pick "Download map." Here WeGo permits you to download whole states or explicit locales in Michigan.

3.   MAPS.ME: This app has detailed maps of the world and was made to be used offline. Search for Michigan in the app store after installing MAPS.ME, and then select the regions you want to download. The application will download the guides to your gadget, and you can get to them whenever even without a web association.

4. Michigan Division of Transportation (MDOT): You can visit the Michigan Department of Transportation website if you prefer official state maps. You might be able to save PDF versions of their maps to your device and use them offline. Highways, cities, landmarks, and recreational areas are often detailed on these maps.

5. OpenStreetMap: OpenStreetMap is a platform for free mapping that lets users download maps and use them offline. Different applications like Maps. me and OsmAnd use OpenStreetMap information. You can download the map in a variety of formats that are compatible with a variety of apps by going to their website and selecting the region of Michigan you want to view.

Tips for downloading maps offline:
- When downloading maps, keep in mind how much space you have on

your device because detailed maps can use a lot of memory.

- Furthermore, it's really smart to download refreshes constantly to guarantee you have the most recent data.

- Download the map before you go to ensure that you always have it with you, even if you don't have access to Wi-Fi or mobile data.

CHAPTER 2

Accomodation and Visas in Michigan

Accommodation in Michigan

There is a wide range of conveniences accessible in Michigan, to suit all financial plans and inclinations. Some of the most well-liked choices are as follows:

1.Hotels: Michigan has hotels for every budget, from low-cost options to luxurious resorts.

2.Motels: Inns are a decent choice for voyagers on a tight spending plan. They commonly offer fundamental facilities, however, they are many times situated close to expressways and other significant transportation centers.

3.Inns and guest houses: Compared to hotels and motels, bed and breakfasts provide a more intimate and familiar setting. They frequently highlight scrumptious morning meals and are situated in enchanting notable structures.

4.Airbnb: Airbnb is an extraordinary choice for explorers who need to remain in a confidential home or condo. This can be an incredible method for encountering neighborhood culture and meeting new individuals.

5.Campgrounds: Michigan has numerous wonderful camping areas, which are an incredible choice for explorers who need to partake in the outside.

Visas for Michigan

The sort of visa you should enter Michigan relies upon your ethnicity and the reason for your visit. The following are some of the most frequently issued visas for Michigan:

1.Visitor's visa: Vacationer visas are for individuals who are visiting Michigan for joy.

2.Business visa: Business visas are for individuals who are visiting Michigan for business purposes.

3.Understudy visa: Understudy visas are for individuals who are concentrating on Michigan.

4.Work visa: Individuals coming to Michigan to work are eligible for work visas.

You can track down more data about visas for Michigan on the site of the US Branch of State.

Entry requirements for Michigan

The passage necessities for Michigan rely upon your ethnicity and the motivation behind your visit. Some general requirements for entering Michigan are as follows:

Passport: You should have a substantial identification that is something like a half-year-old when you enter Michigan.

Visa: You may require a visa to enter Michigan if you are not a citizen of the United States. Your nationality and the purpose of your visit will determine the type of visa you need.

Immunizations: A few nations require specific vaccinations for sections into Michigan. You ought to check with the U.S. Communities for Infectious Prevention and Avoidance (CDC) to check whether you want any inoculations before you travel.

Electronic Framework for Movement Approval (ESTA): Before traveling to Michigan, you will need an ESTA if you are a citizen of a participating nation. The ESTA is an electronic approval that permits you to venture out to the US without a visa for stays of as long as 90 days.

Confirmation of ahead movement: You should have evidence of forward movement, for example, a boarding pass or a transport ticket, when you enter Michigan.

Monetary help: You must demonstrate that you will be able to support yourself while in Michigan.

Great well-being: When you enter Michigan, you must be healthy and free of infectious diseases.

If you don't know whether you meet the section prerequisites for Michigan, you ought to contact the closest U.S. international haven or office.

Resorts and hotels offering affordable rates in Michigan

1. Baymont Mackinaw City by Wyndham: This lodging is situated on Mackinac Island, a vehicle-free island in the Waterways of Mackinac. It has a variety of amenities, including a pool, a hot tub, and a fitness center, as well as affordable rooms and suites.

2. Traverse City's Country Inn & Suites by Radisson: This hotel is in Traverse City, a popular Michigan resort town in the northwest. It has a variety of amenities, including a pool, a hot tub, and a fitness center, as well as affordable rooms and suites.

3. Best Western In addition to Dockside Waterfront Motel: Harbor Springs is a charming town on Lake Michigan and home to this hotel. It has a variety of amenities, including a pool, a hot tub, and a fitness center, as well as affordable rooms and suites.

4. The Holland Hampton Inn: This lodging is situated in Holland, a town on Lake Michigan known for its Dutch legacy. It has a variety of amenities, including a pool, a hot tub, and a fitness center, as well as affordable rooms and suites.

5. Microtel Motel and Suites by Wyndham Ann Arbor: This hotel is in Ann Arbor, Michigan, a college town with a thriving arts scene. It has a variety of amenities, including a pool, a hot tub, and a fitness center, as well as affordable rooms and suites.

These are only a couple of the numerous reasonable retreats and lodgings in Michigan. While picking a lodging, make certain to contrast rates and conveniences with tracking down the best arrangement for your requirements.

Michigan's High-End Hotels & Resorts

Grand Hotel is one of the finest hotels and resorts in Michigan. This notorious lodging is situated on Mackinac Island, a vehicle-free island in the Waterways of Mackinac. It is known for its wonderful Victorian design, its exquisite rooms and suites, and its a-list administration.

1. The Townsend Lodging: This rich lodging is situated in Birmingham, Michigan, a suburb of Detroit. It is known for its modern stylistic layout, its honor winning cafés, and its spa.

2. Grand Plaza Amway Grand Rapids: Michigan is home to this hotel, which is rated five stars by AAA. It has a beautiful lobby, spacious rooms and suites, a spa, a golf course, and a marina, among other amenities.

CHAPTER 3

Michigan's Nightlife and Dining Manners

Nightlife in Michigan

There is something for everyone in Michigan's vibrant nightlife scene. From huge urban communities like Detroit and Fantastic Rapids to humble communities like Cross City and Marquette, there are bars, clubs, and eateries open until quite a bit later.

In Detroit, you'll find everything from stylish mixed drink bars to underground move clubs. There are numerous breweries and brewpubs in Grand Rapids, as well as a lively downtown scene. Wineries, cideries, and restaurants with outdoor seating make Traverse City a more relaxed destination. What's more, Marquette is an incredible spot to go for unrecorded music and school town nightlife.

You'll be able to relax and have a good time no matter where you go in Michigan.

Eating Habits in Michigan

Eating in Michigan is a relaxed undertaking, however, there are a couple of things you ought to remember.

1. Clothing regulation: Most cafés in Michigan have an easygoing clothing standard, yet it's dependably smart to check ahead, particularly if you're anticipating going to a more pleasant eatery.

2. Be on time: It's viewed as impolite to be late for a supper reservation.

3. Be conscious of different coffee shops: Avoid making a scene or talking too loudly.

4. Keep an eye on the things around you: If you're eating in a bustling eatery, be aware of your elbows and other body parts.

5. Tipping: Tipping is normal in Michigan, and the standard is 15-20% of the bill.

6. Social graces: Michiganders are for the most part beautiful and loosened up about social graces, yet there are a couple of things you ought to stay away from. For instance, it's viewed as discourteous to guzzle your soup or talk with your mouth full.

7. Conversation: Don't be afraid to talk to your server or other diners because Michiganders are friendly and outgoing.

Michigan's Foods and Drinks

Michigan has a long and illustrious culinary history, with dishes that reflect the diverse population and geography of the state. Michigan's most popular foods and drinks are as follows:

Coney canines: Coney canines are a Michigan staple, comprising a sausage finished off with bean stew, mustard, and onions. They are a popular snack or meal that is typically served on a steamed bun.

Faygo: Faygo is a famous soda brand that was established in Detroit in 1907. The brand is known for its wide assortment of flavors, including Redpop, Rock and Rye, and Moon Fog.

Chips from Better Quality: Better Made Potato Chips is a chip brand that has been around since 1930 and is based in Michigan. The chips are made with new potatoes and are known for their fresh surface and pungent flavor.

Cross City cherries: Cross City is known for its sweet, tart cherries, which are utilized in various dishes, including pies, shoemakers, and frozen yogurt.

Pizza made in Detroit: Detroit-style pizza is a square pizza that is made with a thick covering and a liberal measure of cheddar. The pizza is ordinarily prepared in a rectangular dish, which gives it its unmistakable firm edges.

Poutine: Poutine is a Canadian dish that is made with french fries, cheddar curds, and sauce. In Michigan, it is a popular late-night snack or meal that can be found at many bars and restaurants.

Michigan lager: With more than 300 breweries located in the state, Michigan is home to a thriving craft beer scene. Michigan lagers are known for their intense flavors and assortment of styles.

These are only a couple of the numerous food sources and beverages that Michigan brings to the table. With its assorted culinary custom, there is something for everybody to appreciate in the Incomparable Lakes State.

The Best Regional Restaurants in Michigan

Michigan is a state with a rich culinary custom, and its local food mirrors the state's different populace and topography. The following are some of Michigan's finest regional eateries:

Szechuan East: This café in Detroit serves true Szechuan cooking. The menu includes a wide assortment of dishes, including map tofu, kung pao chicken, and dan noodles.

Blimpy Burger from Krazy Jim: This burger joint in Ann Arbor is a Michigan organization. The menu has a wide selection of toppings, and the burgers are made with fresh, local ingredients.

The Whitney: This eatery in Detroit serves New American food with an emphasis on neighborhood fixings. The menu changes occasionally, however, you can continuously hope to track down inventive and tasty dishes.

The Bungalow: This café in Navigate City serves exemplary American passage with a contort. The menu highlights dishes like broiled chicken, macintosh and cheddar, and barbecued cheddar sandwiches, yet with a special wind.

The Old Goat: This café in Fantastic Rapids serves gastropub passage with an emphasis on specialty brew. A wide selection of appetizers, salads, sandwiches, and entrees, as well as numerous craft beers available on tap, are on the menu.

Northstar Café: This eatery in Cross City serves upscale American food with an emphasis on privately obtained fixings. The menu includes a wide assortment of dishes, including foie gras, steak, and fish.

Michigan is home to a plethora of excellent regional eateries, such as these. The Great Lakes State has something for everyone thanks to its diverse culinary heritage.

Best cafes and restaurants in Michigan

Cafes:

1. Zola Cafe: This bistro in Ann Arbor is a well-known spot for espresso, cakes, and sandwiches. The bistro is known for its accommodating environment and its delightful food.

2. The Bean Roasted: Coffee, tea, and sandwiches are all excellent options at this Grand Rapids café. Additionally, the cafe offers vegan and gluten-free options.

3. Muse Cafe: This bistro in Navigate City is an extraordinary spot to go for espresso, cakes, and light passage. The cafe has a lovely patio outside where you can watch people go by.

4. The Station of Filling: Breakfast, lunch, and dinner are all excellent options at this Detroit cafe. Sandwiches, salads, and burgers are just a few of the many items on the cafe's menu.

5. The Mudgie's Store: This store in Ann Arbor is a well-known spot for sandwiches, soups, and mixed greens. The shop is known for its new fixings and its imaginative sandwiches.

Restaurants:

1. Selden Standard: New American cuisine with a focus on locally sourced ingredients is served at this Detroit restaurant. The menu changes occasionally, yet you can constantly hope to track down innovative and tasty dishes.

2. The Mechanical Assembly Room: This eatery in Great Rapids serves top-notch food cooking with an emphasis on occasional fixings. The menu changes occasionally, yet you can continuously hope to track down wonderfully introduced and tasty dishes.

3. The Club of Rattlesnakes: Detroit-based upscale American cuisine with a focus on

locally sourced ingredients is served at this restaurant. The menu includes a wide assortment of dishes, including foie gras, steak, and fish.

4. The Gloomy One: This Traverse City restaurant serves New American cuisine that emphasizes locally sourced ingredients. The menu includes a wide assortment of dishes, including cooked chicken, barbecued fish, and pasta dishes.

5. The Boatyard: This café in Saugatuck serves fish with a view. You can enjoy your meal with a view of Lake Michigan because the restaurant is on the shores of the lake.

These are only a couple of the numerous extraordinary bistros and eateries in Michigan. The Great Lakes State has something for everyone thanks to its diverse culinary heritage.

CHAPTER 4

Activities in Michigan

Michigan is a state with a variety of landscapes and activities for tourists to enjoy. The following are a couple of the most famous exercises in Michigan:

Hiking: Michigan has north of 1,000 miles of climbing trails, going from simple to testing. Probably the most famous climbing trails in Michigan incorporate the Dozing Bear Hills Public Lakeshore, the Imagined Rocks Public Lakeshore, and the North Nation Trail.

Camping: Michigan has north of 100 state parks and amusement regions, a considerable lot of which proposition setting up camp. Probably the most well-known camping areas in Michigan incorporate the

Resting Bear Hills Public Lakeshore, the Envisioned Rocks Public Lakeshore, and the Mackinac Island State Park.

Fishing: Michigan is a great place to go fishing because it has more than 11,000 inland lakes and 3,800 miles of rivers. The absolute most famous fish to get in Michigan incorporate salmon, trout, bass, and walleye.

Aquatic sports: As a state on the Great Lakes, Michigan offers numerous opportunities for water sports like kayaking, sailing, swimming, and boating. Probably the most well-known water sports objections in Michigan incorporate Lake Michigan, Lake Huron, and the Detroit Stream.

Winter sports: Michigan has various extraordinary ski resorts, ideal for skiing, snowboarding, and snowshoeing. Probably the most well-known ski resorts in Michigan incorporate Boyne Mountain, Precious Stone Mountain, and Mount Brighton.

Observing wildlife: Wildlife abounds in Michigan, including eagles, bears, deer, and wolves. Probably the best places to go for untamed life seeing in Michigan incorporate the Resting Bear Rises Public Lakeshore, the Imagined Rocks Public Lakeshore, and the Huron Public Woods.

These are only a couple of the many energizing outside exercises you can appreciate in Michigan. With its dazzling regular magnificence, fluctuating landscape, and four unmistakable seasons, Michigan is an expression that brings something to the table for everybody.

Michigan's Educational Attractions and Museums

The following Michigan attractions and museums offer educational value:

1. Exhibits on American culture, innovation, and history are on display at the Henry Ford Museum in Dearborn, a vast museum complex. The historical center is home to a copy of Thomas Edison's lab, a Model T sequential construction system, and an assortment of one-of-a-kind vehicles.

2. The Detroit Establishment of Expressions is a workmanship historical center in Detroit with an assortment of north of 65,000 masterpieces, including canvases, figures, and beautiful expressions. The exhibition hall is home to works by a portion of the world's most popular craftsmen, including Vincent van Gogh, Claude Monet, and Pablo Picasso.

3. There are exhibits on technology, space, and natural history at the science museum in Bloomfield Hills called the Cranbrook Institute of Science. The exhibition hall is home to a planetarium, a butterfly garden, and an involved science place.

4. The Michigan Science Center in Detroit is a science gallery with displays on various logical subjects, including physical science, science, and design. A planetarium, an IMAX theater, and a hands-on science center are all found in the museum.

5. The Ann Arbor Involved Gallery in Ann Arbor is a kids' historical center with displays that urge youngsters to learn through play. The gallery is home to different intelligent displays, including a water table, a development zone, and a supermarket.

6. The Frederik Meijer Gardens and Figure Park in Fantastic Rapids is a greenhouse and model park with north of 1,000 sections of land of nurseries, backwoods, and knolls. Several sculptures, including pieces by Henry Moore, Alexander Calder, and Louise Bourgeois, can be found in the garden.

7. The Dozing Bear Rises Public Lakeshore in Realm is a public lakeshore with transcending sand hills, unblemished sea shores, and lavish backwoods. There are numerous camping areas, beaches, and hiking trails in the park.

These are only a couple of the numerous historical centers and attractions in Michigan with instructive worth. With its rich history, various cultures, and staggering normal magnificence, Michigan is an expression that brings something to the table for everybody.

Visiting Zoos and Wildlife in Michigan

Here are a few insights concerning visiting zoos and untamed life in Michigan:

Zoos: The John Ball Zoo, the Detroit Zoo, and the Binder Park Zoo are all excellent zoos in Michigan. These zoos offer guests the chance to see different creatures from everywhere in the world, including lions, tigers, bears, elephants, and giraffes. Numerous zoos likewise offer instructive projects and exercises, making them an incredible spot to find out about creatures and their environments.

Wilderness areas: The Seney National Wildlife Refuge, the Huron National Forest, and the Manistee National Forest are just a few of the many wildlife refuges in Michigan. Deer, bears, wolves, and eagles are just a few of the many species of wildlife that can be found in these refuges. These locations are ideal for wildlife viewing because visitors frequently have the opportunity to observe these animals in their natural environments.

State parks: Michigan likewise has north of 100 state parks, large numbers of which offer chances to see natural life. The absolute best state parks for natural life see incorporate the Dozing Bear Rises Public Lakeshore, the Imagined Rocks Public Lakeshore, and the Huron Public Woods.

Michigan is home to the following zoos and wildlife parks:

Plan your visit: Check the website of the zoo or wildlife refuge before you go to see what animals are on display and what activities are available. This will assist you with arranging your visit and capitalize on your time.

Be conscious: While visiting zoos and natural life asylums, make certain to be aware of the creatures and their living spaces. Try not to take care of the creatures, don't make clear commotions, and don't get excessively near the creatures.

Take as much time as is needed: Your visit to a zoo or wildlife refuge should not be rushed. Take as much time as necessary, notice the creatures, and find out about their living spaces.

Michigan's Best Beaches

It should come as no surprise that Michigan has some of the best beaches in the country because the state has more than 3,000 miles of coastline. The following are a couple of the first-class sea shores in Michigan:

National Park Sleeping Bear Dunes: This public lakeshore is home to the absolute most lovely sea shores in Michigan, including Domain Oceanside, Glen Arbor Oceanside, and South Manitou Island Oceanside. The seashores are known for their delicate sand, clear waters, and shocking perspectives on the hills.

Island of Mackinac: This vehicle-free island is known for its beguiling shops, noteworthy Fantastic Inn, and wonderful seashores. Swimming, sunbathing, and exploring are all possible on Mackinac Island's beaches.

State Park of Grand Haven: This state park is home to an extended length of sandy ocean side that is ideal for swimming, sunbathing, and surfing. The recreation area likewise has various conveniences, including a jungle gym, outing regions, and a snack bar.

Park P.J. Hoffmaster State: A stunning beach with numerous dunes and crystal-clear waters can be found in this state park. The recreation area likewise has various conveniences, including a jungle gym, cookout regions, and a snack bar.

State Park Warren Dunes: This state park is great for hiking, sand sledding, and exploring because it is home to some of Michigan's tallest dunes. Additionally, the park has several beaches that are ideal for fishing, swimming, and sunbathing.

These are only a couple of the numerous extraordinary seashores in Michigan. With its dazzling normal magnificence, fluctuated landscape, and four particular seasons, Michigan is an expression that brings something to the table for everybody.

Here are a few ways to visit Michigan's seashores:

Plan your visit: Check the beach's website before you go to see what amenities are available and what the weather is going to be like. This will assist you with arranging your visit and taking advantage of your time.

Respect others: While visiting Michigan's seashores, make certain to be deferential to the climate. In protected areas, don't litter, don't disturb the wildlife, and don't build sandcastles.

Give it some time: You shouldn't rush through your time at a Michigan beach. Take your time, unwind, and take in the state's natural splendor.

In-demand parks in Michigan

Michigan has more than 100 state parks, and every one offers exceptional excellence and attractions. In Michigan, some of the most popular parks include:

Dozing Bear Rises Public Lakeshore: Towering dunes, pristine beaches, and lush forests make up this national lakeshore. Hiking, camping, swimming, and fishing are all popular activities in the park.

State Park of Tahquamenon Falls: This park is home to two of the biggest cascades in the Eastern US. Fishing, hiking, and camping are all popular activities in the park.

Mackinac Island State Park: 74% of Mackinac Island, a car-free island in the Straits of Mackinac, is covered by this park. The recreation area is home to delightful seashores, climbing trails, and memorable destinations.

State Park in the Porcupine Mountains Wilderness: This park is home to north of 100 miles of climbing trails, as well as cascades, lakes, and woods. The recreation area is a well-known objective for hiking, setting up camp, and fishing.

Warren Rises State Park: This park is home to probably the tallest sand ridges in Michigan, making it an extraordinary spot for climbing, sand sledding, and investigating. The recreation area likewise has various seashores that are ideal for swimming, sunbathing, and fishing.

These are just a few of Michigan's many popular parks. With its dazzling regular excellence, fluctuated landscape, and four unmistakable seasons, Michigan is an expression that brings something to the table for everybody.

The following are some pointers for visiting Michigan's popular parks:

Make a visit plan: Before you go, really take a look at the recreation area's site to see what conveniences are accessible and what the weather conditions estimate is. This will assist you with arranging your visit and capitalize on your time.

Respect others: While visiting Michigan's sought-after parks, make certain to be aware of the climate. Try not to litter, don't upset the natural life, and don't construct sandcastles in safeguarded regions.

Take as much time as is needed: You shouldn't rush through your visit to a popular park in Michigan. Take as much time as is needed, unwind, and partake in the magnificence of the state.

Cultural Activities in Michigan

The Henry Passage Gallery: This historical center complex in Dearborn is home to various shows on American history, advancement, and culture. A Model T assembly line, a replica of Thomas Edison's laboratory, and a collection of vintage automobiles are all housed in the museum.

The Detroit Organization of Expressions: Over 65,000 pieces of art, including paintings, sculptures, and decorative arts, are on display at this Detroit museum. The historical center is home to works by a portion of the world's most popular specialists, including Vincent van Gogh, Claude Monet, and Pablo Picasso.

The Cranbrook Organization of Science: This science historical center in Bloomfield Slopes has shows on normal history, space, and innovation. A hands-on science center, a butterfly garden, and a planetarium are all found in the museum.

The Michigan Center for Science: This Detroit science museum has exhibits on physics, biology, and engineering, among other scientific fields. A planetarium, an IMAX theater, and a hands-on science center are all found in the museum.

The Hands-On Museum in Ann Arbor: This youngsters' historical center in Ann Arbor has displays that urge kids to learn through play. A grocery store, a construction zone, and a water table are among the museum's interactive exhibits.

The Frederik Meijer Gardens and Model Park: This professional flowerbed and model park in Terrific Rapids has more than 1,000 sections of land for nurseries, backwoods, and knolls. Several sculptures, including pieces by Henry Moore, Alexander Calder, and Louise Bourgeois, can be found in the garden.

The Detroit Drama House: Opera, ballet, and theater performances all take place at this Detroit opera house. The opera house is a popular venue for cultural events and is a stunning example of 19th-century architecture.

The Fox Cinema: This Detroit theater hosts a wide range of performances, including comedy acts, Broadway shows, and concerts. The theater is a delightful illustration of Craftsmanship Deco engineering and is a famous objective for widespread developments.

These are only a couple of the numerous social exercises in Michigan. Michigan is a state that has something for everyone thanks to its diverse culture, rich history, and stunning natural beauty.

CHAPTER 5

Transportation options: Buses, trains, and ferries are just a few of the public transportation options available in Michigan. The expense of public transportation fluctuates relying upon the distance voyaged and the kind of transportation utilized.

Cabs and ride-flagging down administrations: Cabs and ride-flagging down administrations are accessible in most significant urban communities in Michigan. The distance traveled and the time of day affect the cost of taxis and ride-hailing services.

Vehicle rental: Michigan is a popular destination for renting a car. The expense of vehicle rental differs depending upon the kind of vehicle leased, the length of the rental, and the season.

Bicycle: During the summer, biking is a great way to get around Michigan. There are many bicycle trails and ways all through the state. Biking is completely free.

Walking: Strolling is an extraordinary method for getting around Michigan, particularly in more modest towns and urban communities. Walking is completely free.

The expense of transportation in Michigan shifts relying upon the method of transportation utilized and the distance voyaged. As a rule, the expense of public transportation is less expensive than the expense of vehicle rental or cabs. Walking and biking are both free.

Here are a few ways to get a good deal on transportation in Michigan:

Utilize public transportation: Public transportation is an extraordinary cash-saving tip for transportation in Michigan.

Exploit limits: Seniors, students, and people with disabilities can take advantage of discounts on numerous public transportation systems.

Carpool or vanpool: Carpooling or vanpooling is an incredible cash-saving tip for gas and stopping.

Walk or bicycle: Strolling and trekking are free and an incredible method for getting some activity.

Shopping in Michigan

Transportation options: Buses, trains, and ferries are just a few of the public transportation options available in Michigan. The expense of public transportation fluctuates relying upon the distance voyaged and the kind of transportation utilized.

Cabs and ride-flagging down administrations: Cabs and ride-flagging down administrations are accessible in most significant urban communities in Michigan. The distance traveled and the time of day affect the cost of taxis and ride-hailing services.

Vehicle rental: Michigan is a popular destination for renting a car. The expense of vehicle rental differs depending upon the kind of vehicle leased, the length of the rental, and the season.

Bicycle: During the summer, biking is a great way to get around Michigan. There are many bicycle trails and ways all through the state. Biking is completely free.

Walking: Strolling is an extraordinary method for getting around Michigan, particularly in more modest towns and urban communities. Walking is completely free.

The expense of transportation in Michigan shifts relying upon the method of transportation utilized and the distance voyaged. As a rule, the expense of public transportation is less expensive than the expense of vehicle rental or cabs. Walking and biking are both free.

Here are a few ways to get a good deal on transportation in Michigan:

Utilize public transportation: Public transportation is an extraordinary cash-saving tip for transportation in Michigan.

Exploit limits: Seniors, students, and people with disabilities can take advantage of discounts on numerous public transportation systems.

Carpool or vanpool: Carpooling or vanpooling is an incredible cash-saving tip for gas and stopping.

Walk or bicycle: Strolling and trekking are free and an incredible method for getting some activity.

Top 6 Must-Know Pre-Visit Tips for a First-Time Traveler to Michigan

On the off chance that you're arranging your most memorable outing to Michigan, here are the main six must-know pre-visit tips to guarantee a smooth and charming experience:

1.   Examination and Plan Ahead: Before relying on your Michigan experience, direct careful exploration about the state's attractions, climate, and social features.

Make a nitty gritty schedule in light of your inclinations and inclinations. Michigan offers a different scope of encounters, from investigating the clamoring city life of Detroit to loosening up on the tranquil shores of Lake Michigan. Plan your outing in a manner to capitalize on your time in the Incomparable Lakes State.

2.   Pack As needs be for the Climate: Michigan encounters each of the four particular seasons, and the weather conditions can be eccentric, particularly close to the Incomparable Lakes. Pack clothing appropriate for the season you'll visit, including layers for momentary seasons like spring and fall. If you intend to travel to the northern regions or participate in winter sports, be prepared for snow and cold temperatures during the winter. In the late spring, bring sunscreen, caps, and lightweight attire for hotter days.

3.   Find the Incomparable Lakes:

One of Michigan's most popular tourist attractions is its Great Lakes. If you intend to visit Lake Michigan or Lake Unrivaled, make a point to bring beachwear, as the sandy shores are ideally suited for ocean-side exercises and unwinding. If you're going with kids, consider seeing family-accommodating seashores and waterfront parks for a sensational day by the water.

4. Explore Outdoor Activities and Nature:

Take advantage of Michigan's unparalleled natural beauty by planning outdoor activities. Climbing in state parks like Dozing Bear Rises Public Lakeshore or the Porcupine Mountains Wild State Park will compensate you with dazzling vistas and noteworthy encounters. On the off chance that you appreciate water sports, consider kayaking or paddleboarding on the inland lakes or investigating the beautiful streams. Furthermore, don't botch the valuable chance to observe the fall foliage, particularly assuming that you're visiting during pre-winter.

5. Take Advantage of Michigan's Delicious Foods:

Michigan's assorted social legacy is reflected in its culinary scene. Enjoy territorial top choices, for example, Coney canines in Detroit, pasties in the Upper Landmass, and cherry-propelled dishes in Navigate City. Ranchers markets across the state offer new produce and nearby strengths. Remember to test the prestigious Michigan specialty lagers and wines, as the state is home to numerous microbreweries and wineries.

6. Make yourself familiar with the culture:

Before you visit Michigan, find out more about neighborhood customs and practices. Accept the local culture and interact with the people there because Michiganders are known for their friendliness and openness.

Keep in mind the Leave No Trace principles when exploring nature to preserve the state's natural beauty for future generations.

Day Trips & Excursions in Michigan

Michigan is a great place for both locals and tourists because it has so many day trips and excursions that cater to a wide range of interests. Whether you're hoping to investigate clamoring urban communities, loosen up on sandy sea shores, submerge yourself in nature, or dive into social and authentic milestones, Michigan brings something to the table for each explorer. We should dive into a portion of the top road trips and trips in the Incomparable Lakes State:

1. Island of Mackinac:

A road trip to Mackinac Island is a stage back in time. Open by ship from Mackinaw City or St. Ignace, the island is renowned for its all-around safeguarded Victorian engineering, horse-drawn carriages, and shocking normal magnificence. Investigate the memorable Post Mackinac, respect the Terrific Inn's famous engineering, and lease a bicycle to ride around the island to observe its beautiful scenes. Mackinac Island has no mechanized vehicles, making an extraordinary and serene air.

2. Cross City and Dozing Bear Hills: Traverse City, which is on the shores of Lake Michigan, is well-known for its cherry orchards, wineries, and thriving arts scene. Require a road trip to investigate the region's picturesque excellence, visit wineries along the Old Mission Landmass or the Leelanau Promontory Wine Trail, and enjoy nearby culinary joys. Close by, the Dozing Bear Ridges Public Lakeshore offers lofty sand hills and flawless sea shores, giving sufficient chances to climb, picnicking, and absorbing all-encompassing perspectives.

3. Detroit:

Detroit, the largest city in Michigan, is a great destination for a day trip because of its many cultural and tourist attractions. Visit the Detroit Organization of Expressions, home to an amazing assortment of fine art from various periods and societies. Find the city's rich melodic legacy at the Motown Gallery or submerge yourself throughout the entire existence of the auto business at the Henry Portage Exhibition Hall and Greenfield Town. Try not to miss a walk around the revived Detroit Riverfront or test the city's blossoming culinary scene.

4. Ann Arbor:

Known for its energetic school town air, Ann Arbor is home to the College of Michigan and offers a superb road trip objective. Take a look around the campus and its famous buildings, like Michigan Stadium (the Big House). Meander through the beguiling midtown loaded up with one-of-a-kind shops, craftsmanship displays, and eateries.

The Nichols Arboretum and Matthaei Botanical Gardens offer tranquil natural areas for exploration and relaxation.

5.   Holland and Terrific Asylum:

Take a day trip to Holland to experience Dutch culture. Visit the Dutch Village, a recreation of a traditional Dutch town, as you stroll the streets lined with tulips. With parades, Dutch dancing, and cultural events, the Tulip Time Festival celebrates the blooming of thousands of tulips in the spring. Close by, Great Shelter is well known for its sandy sea shores, beacons, and the notable melodic wellspring, a synchronized water and light show.

6.   Waterfalls   in   the   Upper Peninsula:

A day trip to the Upper Peninsula in Michigan will show you some of the most stunning waterfalls in the state. There are waterfalls, vibrant sandstone cliffs, and a pristine   lakeshore   at   Pictured   Rocks

National Lakeshore. In addition, Bond Falls and Tahquamenon Falls are must-see destinations for their breathtaking waterfalls. Consolidate your cascade experience with a climb in the state and public parks for an extraordinary day in nature.

7. South Haven and Saugatuck:

Saugatuck and South Haven, two charming beach towns on Lake Michigan's eastern shore, are ideal for a leisurely day trip. There are a lot of art galleries and boutiques in Saugatuck, and South Haven has sandy beaches and a pretty lighthouse. Appreciate beachcombing, take a ridge buggy ride, and relish the nearby kinds of these great Lake Michigan towns.

8. Frankenmuth:

Known as Michigan's Little Bavaria, Frankenmuth is an interesting German-themed town with beguiling engineering, one-of-a-kind shops, and eateries serving Bavarian cooking. Take a relaxing boat cruise on the Cass River to see the town's scenic beauty and visit Bronner's Christmas Wonderland, the largest Christmas store in the world.

These are just a few of Michigan's many exciting day trips and excursions. Whether you're keen on history, nature, culture, or essentially need to loosen up near the ocean, Michigan's different objections guarantee there's continuously a novel, new thing to investigate only a road trip away.

CHAPTER 6

Suggested itineraries for Michigan

Agenda 1: The Upper Landmass

The Upper Landmass (UP) is a delightful and rough district of Michigan that is home to staggering landscapes, enchanting towns, and a lot of outside exercises. For a five-day trip to the UP, a suggested itinerary is as follows:

Day 1: Marquette, the largest city in the UP, is a good place to start your day. Visit the Marquette Maritime Museum, the city's historic downtown, or Sugarloaf Mountain for stunning views of the city and Lake Superior.

Day 2: Take a drive to Munising, a small town on Lake Superior's shores. In the Pictured Rocks National Lakeshore, you can go kayaking or stand-up paddleboarding, hike to the top of Miners' Castle, or visit the Grand Sable Dunes.

Day 3: Drive to the small town of Copper Harbor, which is on the tip of the Keweenaw Peninsula. Investigate the town's noteworthy mining region, go climbing in the Porcupine Mountains Wild State Park, or take a boat visit through the harbor.

Day 4: Drive to Sault Ste. Marie, a city on the line between the U.S. what's more, Canada. Pay a visit to the Soo Locks, a collection of locks that enable ships to travel between Lake Huron and Lake Superior. Take a boat visit through the locks, or visit the Sault Ste. to learn more about the city's past at the Marie Museum.

Day 5: Return by car to either Mackinac Island or Marquette. Visit the Au Sable Lighthouse and hike to the top of Chapel Rock at Pictured Rocks National Lakeshore if you have time.

Agenda 2: The Lower Promontory

The Lower Promontory is home to a portion of Michigan's most well-known vacation locations, including Detroit, Ann Arbor, and Mackinac Island. Here is a recommended schedule for a 5-road trip to the Lower Landmass:

Day 1: Detroit, Michigan's largest city, is a great place to start your day. Take a stroll through Detroit's historic downtown, the Henry Ford Museum, or the Detroit Institute of Arts.

Day 2: Take a drive to Ann Arbor, a college town known for its lively downtown and vibrant arts scene. Visit the College of Michigan grounds, go out to shop on Central Avenue, or catch a show at the Ann Arbor Summer Celebration.

Day 3: Drive to Mackinac Island, a vehicle-free island in Lake Huron. Investigate the island's memorable midtown, climb to the highest point of Post Mackinac, or take a carriage ride around the island.

Day 4: Drive to Traverse City, a town on Lake Michigan's shores. Go wine sampling in the Leelanau Promontory, visit the Resting Bear Hills Public Lakeshore, or take a boat visit through the Excellent Navigate Straight.

Day 5: Drive back to Detroit or Chicago. If you have time, stop at the Resting Bear Ridges Public Lakeshore to climb to the highest point of Pyramid Point or visit the Glen Arbor Ocean side.

These are just a few suggestions for Michigan travel routes. Feel free to look around and make your itinerary because the state has a lot of great places to visit

Practices for Sustainable Tourism

A mode of travel that minimizes adverse effects on society, the environment, and culture is known as sustainable tourism. There are numerous ways of rehearsing feasible the travel industry in Michigan, including:

- Remaining in eco-accommodating facilities. There are numerous lodgings, overnight boarding houses, and getaway rentals in Michigan that are focused on maintainability. These organizations might utilize energy-effective machines, reused materials, and water-saving apparatuses. They may likewise offer to reuse and fertilize the soil projects, and they might uphold nearby organizations and ranchers.

- Preparing for your trip in advance You can choose activities and destinations that are less likely to harm the environment if you plan your trip. You can, for instance, choose to go to national parks and other protected areas or engage in low-impact activities like camping, biking, and hiking.

- Regarding the climate. Respecting the environment is essential when traveling. This implies abandoning no follow, discarding waste appropriately, and staying away from exercises that could harm regular assets. It also means respecting wildlife and their natural surroundings.

- Supporting neighborhood organizations. You can help the local economy and reduce your carbon footprint by supporting local businesses. Local businesses are more likely to support local farmers and other businesses and to use sustainable methods.

- Finding out about the nearby culture. At the point when you travel, finding out about the nearby culture is significant. Respecting local traditions and supporting local businesses and organizations are two aspects of this. It likewise implies finding out about the set of experiences and environment of the locale.

By following these practices, you can assist in guaranteeing that your movements in Michigan are reasonable and that you are decidedly affecting the climate, society, and culture.

Additional suggestions for Michigan's sustainable tourism include the following:

- Pack light. The lighter your baggage, the less fuel you will use to ship it.

- Bring reusable water containers and utensils. This will assist with diminishing waste.

- Consume local fare. This will uphold nearby ranchers and diminish your carbon impression.

- Go by open transportation or bicycle. This will assist with diminishing air contamination.

- Know about your effect on untamed life. Try not to upset creatures or their environments.

Leave no follow. This implies pressing out the entirety of your waste and regarding the climate.

Emergency Line in Michigan

911: In the United States, this number is used for all emergencies. You can call 911 from any telephone, regardless of whether you have an arrangement or on the other hand if your telephone isn't charged. 911 is for announcing crises, like flames, wrongdoings, and health-related crises.

311: This is a non-crisis number that can be utilized to report different issues, like potholes, spray painting, and deserted vehicles. Although 311 is not for reporting emergencies, it can be a convenient way to get help with issues that aren't emergencies.

Michigan State Police: You can get in touch with the Michigan State Police at 517-332-2521. The MSP can be contacted for traffic accidents, criminal investigations, and missing person reports, among other law enforcement matters.

Michigan Branch of Wellbeing and Human Administrations: The Michigan Division of Wellbeing and Human Administrations can be reached at 800-678-8914. The MDHHS can be reached for various well-being and human administration matters, including emotional well-being emergencies, youngster misuse, and senior maltreatment.

Notwithstanding these crisis numbers, there are likewise various specialty hotlines that can be utilized to report explicit sorts of crises. For instance, the Public Self-destruction Avoidance Help can be reached at 1-800-273-8255. The Public Rape Hotline can be reached at 1-800-656-Trust.

It is critical to recall that calling 911 is generally the most ideal choice assuming you are encountering a crisis. Be that as it may, if you don't know whether you are encountering a crisis, you can constantly call 311 or the proper specialty hotline for help.

Here are a few extra ways to call crisis lines in Michigan:

- Be collected and speak clearly. The nature of your emergency and your location will be required by the dispatcher.

- Give however much data as could be expected. This incorporates the area of the crisis, the number of individuals included, and the seriousness of the circumstance.

- Pay attention to the dispatcher's directions. You will be instructed by the dispatcher to proceed.

- Unless the dispatcher tells you to, do not hang up. The dispatcher may need to ask you more questions or give you more instructions.

By following these tips, you can assist in guaranteeing that your call to a crisis line is as successful as could be expected.

Reviewing My Michigan Experience

- What did you appreciate most about your time in Michigan?

- Was it the normal magnificence, the amicable individuals, or the different scope of exercises and attractions?

- What was a portion of the difficulties you confronted?

- Did it have to do with the weather, the high cost of living, or the lack of diversity?

- What advice would you give to others considering a trip to Michigan?

- What are the best places to stay, the best places to see, and the must-see places?

- How did your involvement with Michigan alter your viewpoint on the state?

- Did you learn anything new about Michigan's set of experiences, culture, or individuals?

- What were your assumptions for your excursion? Is it true that they met?

- What were some of your favorite trip memories?

- What might you do another way if you could return?

- Would you refer others to Michigan?

You can gain a deeper understanding of what Michigan has to offer and determine whether it is a place you would like to return to by reflecting on your experience there.

Here are a few ways to compose a survey of your Michigan experience:

- Tell the truth and be fair-minded. Give your honest thoughts and feelings—both positive and negative—about your trip.

- Be explicit. Try not to simply say that you partook in your time in Michigan. Describe in detail what you liked and didn't like about the experience.

- Help out. Others planning a trip to Michigan should find your review useful. Share your suggestions and advice.

- Be locking in. Your audit ought to be fascinating to pursue. Utilize distinctive language and narrating strategies to rejuvenate your experience.

By following these tips, you can compose a survey of your Michigan experience that is both enlightening and locking in.

Conclusion

Congrats on finishing your excursion through the dazzling pages of the "Michigan Travel Guide"! We hope this book has piqued your interest in and wanderlust for the Great Lakes State as you close it.

Michigan is a gold mine of encounters, ready to be uncovered by brave pilgrims like you. From the clamoring roads of Detroit to the peaceful shores of Lake Michigan, each edge of this delightful state has a story to tell.

Whether you're a nature devotee looking for picturesque vistas and cascades, a set of experiences buff submerging yourself in the stories of the past, or a foodie taking pleasure in the local luxuries, Michigan greets you wholeheartedly.

Keep in mind, the experience doesn't end here! Start your individual Michigan odyssey with the insights, hints, and hidden gems in this guide. Make recollections, fashion associations with the cordial local people, and value the minutes that make your excursion remarkable.

Let Michigan's scenic beauty and charm make a lasting impression on your heart as you wander its landscapes. And if you ever find yourself longing to return, keep in mind that Michigan's allure is never-ending, beckoning you back for more memorable adventures.

Presently, with the "Michigan Travel Guide" as your dependable buddy, the potential outcomes are huge. Therefore, pack your belongings, set your compass, and follow your wanderlust. Michigan is ready to show you its magic one adventure at a time, and it is waiting for you with open arms.

Welcome aboard and have fun on your trip to Michigan!

Printed in Great Britain
by Amazon

44819341R00076